The Law Dawg's Common Sense Guide to Special Education Law

THE LAW DAWG'S

Common Sense Guide to Special Education Law

Ten Steps Toward a More Effective Special Education Program

SECOND EDITION

Jim Walsh

Park Place Publications, L.P.
Austin, Texas

First edition published 2006. Second edition 2012.

512 W Martin Luther King Jr Blvd, #300
Austin, TX 78701
512-478-2133 • Fax: 512-495-9955
www.ed311.com

Second Edition
First Printing: August 2012
Second Printing: January 2015
Third Printing: August 2015
Fourth Printing: September 2016
Fifth Printing: March 2018
Sixth Printing: June 2019
Seventh Printing: May 2021
ISBN 978-0-9833083-7-9

Dedication

This book is dedicated to all of those educators who fight the good fight on a daily basis, seeking better services for the kids in our public schools. Some of these people work in the special education department. Some work in the general education department. All of them work for a better future for the students they serve, and for all of us. They deserve our respect and our support.

Acknowledgments

I hope that readers will find this Common Sense Guide to be just that—a helpful resource with some practical, common sense suggestions. Much of what you will read here represents accrued experience over many years of working with educators and lawyers, trying to navigate the sometimes troubled waters where law and education intersect. There are too many people who have taught me and inspired me to be listed here. But I will particularly mention two groups—one from the legal world and one from the educational world.

As for the lawyers, I have been privileged to be a part of the law firm of Walsh, Anderson, Gallegos, Green & Treviño. Walsh Anderson attorneys dedicate themselves to helping the people who help the kids. As such, we believe we are part of the solution. My colleagues and partners at Walsh Anderson are as fine a group of people as I have ever known.

In the educational world, I must particularly single out the special education directors of Texas. I have seen their jobs get much more complex over the years I have worked with them. With complexity comes stress. Besides continuing to serve their districts and the students, the directors have been tremendously supportive and encouraging to me as I help them to understand and apply the law to ever changing situations.

I hope you enjoy the second edition of this Common Sense Guide. It has been a pleasure to get all these thoughts down on paper.

Jim Walsh

August 2012

The Law Dawg's Common Sense Guide to Special Education Law

This book is for "special ed types" as well as others. I began associating with "special ed types" many years ago when I figured out that "special ed" was going to be where the action was, legally speaking. I have now spent so much time with special ed types that I have become one. I even have developed a quiz to determine whether or not a person is a special ed type. Ready for the quiz? Here goes:

The Special Ed Type Quiz

A special education director calls me for some advice regarding a student who is struggling in school. The director says, "He's not doing very well and we're concerned about him, but we don't know what to do with him. We've looked into all of our special programs and he doesn't seem to qualify. We've studied the rules and regulations and consulted with every expert we could think of. Do you have any suggestions?"

I then tell the director: "Well, it sounds to me like you thought the kid might be ED, LD or OHI due to ADD or ADHD, MR or TBI. I'm sure you did want to come up with an IEP so that you could provide FAPE in the LRE, and thus comply with IDEA. And I expect you also considered OT, PT and all sorts of ATDs. I'm guessing you've looked at the DOE, OCR and SEA guidelines and probably also thought about making AYP under NCLB with an HQ teacher Finally, you likely FIE'd him, you IEP'd, 504'd him and DNQ'd him. I'd say the K-I-D is O-U-T!"

Scoring: If you understood 80 percent of the above, you are most definitely a special ed type!

Whether or not you scored 80 percent, I hope that you find this little book to be helpful. Students with disabilities comprise about 10 percent of the student population, but they generate a disproportionate percentage of legal concerns. There are more rules, laws, procedures and accountability measures attached to these students than any other group. Thus, "special ed types" are well aware how complicated it is to run a good special education program today as compared to those in years past.

When life gets complicated, it is a good idea to try to simplify without being simplistic. That is precisely what I have attempted to do in this book — to provide a set of 10 simple steps, all of which are designed to help you comply with the law *and* serve your students better. The thought behind this approach is that:

IF WE SERVE STUDENTS BETTER,
PARENTS WILL BE HAPPY.
TEACHERS WILL BE HAPPY.
WE WILL HAVE FEWER LEGAL PROBLEMS.
WE CAN FOCUS ON SERVING STUDENTS BETTER.

1

STEP ONE

DEFINE WHAT SPECIAL EDUCATION IS AND WHAT IT IS NOT.

The term "special ed" is not well-defined in the minds of educators. I remember clearly the time when I was in a bar with a group of special education directors, diagnosticians and other such types when we apparently got a bit rowdy. The waitress approached our table and inquired, "Who are you people?" Without hesitation and in unison the group responded, "We're special ed!"

Well, of course, *we* were not special ed. But you have to wonder what our waitress must have thought.

To find out what special education really means, we do not need to go to a dictionary or an educational treatise. We need to go to the law. Once a term is defined in the law, the legal definition becomes the trump card. In 1975, Congress got involved in special education with the passage of Public Law 94-142, the predecessor to what we now call IDEA (Individuals with Disabilities Education Act). Thus for almost 40 years now, terms that formerly were the exclusive province of educators have become a part of our law, to be further defined by judges.

The legal definition of "special education" can be found at 20 U.S.C. 1401(29):

The term "special education" means specially designed instruction, at no cost to parents, to meet the unique needs of a child with a disability, including—

(A) instruction conducted in the classroom, in the home, in hospitals and institutions, and in other settings; and

(B) instruction in physical education.

While that definition leaves many questions unanswered, it is the necessary starting point because it is the law.

From the statute passed by Congress, we next turn to regulations adopted by the Department of Education. The entire regulation is lengthy, but for our purposes, I want to hone in on a crucial part of the regulatory definition:

> *Specially designed instruction means adapting as appropriate to the needs of an eligible child under this part, the content, methodology, or delivery of instruction—*
>
> *(i) to address the unique needs of the child that result from the child's disability; and*
>
> *(ii) to ensure access of the child to the general curriculum, so that he or she can meet the educational standards within the jurisdiction of the public agency that apply to all children.* 34 C.F.R. 300.26(b)(3)

Putting these definitions together, we can reach several important conclusions about what special education really means.

1. Special education is all about INSTRUCTION. Noninstructional services, such as occupational therapy, physical therapy and school health services, are not special ed.
2. Special education is about having to CHANGE something. Notice that the definition of "specially designed instruction" (SDI) uses the term "adapting." When you provide special education, you must be adapting or changing what you normally do or how you normally do it.
3. You cannot know that you are changing something if you do not have a good sense of what you normally do or how you normally do it. So, to define special education, you first must define "general education."
4. Special education involves changing one of three specific things: the CONTENT, the

METHODOLOGY or the DELIVERY of instruction. Changes in content are the easiest to identify, because most states have adopted standards setting out what students are expected to learn at each grade level. However, changes in methodology and delivery of instruction are not as readily recognizable and require some work at the district level. What is your customary methodology? How do you normally deliver instruction?

5. Special education involves changing what you do or how you do it FOR A SPECIFIC REASON: "to meet the unique needs of a child with a disability." So, special ed is specifically focused on a student's educational needs, which arise from the disability. Congress is not using the word "unique" in the traditional "one of a kind" sense here. Rather, Congress is saying that special education must address needs that *are unique to the disability*. Notice that the regulation

makes this a bit clearer: "to address the unique needs of the child that *result from* the child's disability."

6. This clearly implies that changes in content, methodology or delivery that are provided for reasons *other than* the child's disability do not qualify as special education. This is not to say that these changes should not be provided; it's simply stating that they do not qualify as "special education" as the term is used in the law. Bilingual education is not "special ed." Remediation courses for general education students are not "special ed."

Special education services can be designed to help specific students meet the same academic standards applicable to all students. Notice that the regulation calls for ensuring "access to the general curriculum, so that he or she can meet the educational standards … that apply to all children." In this case, it seems logical that special education teachers would make changes in methodology or delivery, rather than content. If the student is expected to meet the same standards as the general education students, then the content of instruction is not being changed.

These legal and regulatory definitions are helpful, but they still fail to tell the whole story. To define special ed, some work remains to be done at the local level. While the CONTENT of instruction is defined by state law, the METHODOLOGY and DELIVERY is very much left up to the individual school district.

My suggestion is to create a task force in your school district to further define special education. The task force should be comprised of veteran educators — general ed teachers, special ed teachers and curriculum specialists — with all grade levels represented. The task force's goal is to provide a clear line of demarcation between "special ed" and "general ed" with regard to methodology and delivery. Keep in mind that classroom instruction is not a mechanical process; teachers are not robots. Everyone has their unique way of doing things. Therefore, not every variation on custom is a change in methodology or delivery.

Furthermore, there are some changes in methodology or delivery that most school districts would expect teachers to make for students, even when no disability is present. Teachers are expected to take into account individual differences in learners and tailor instruction accordingly. So, your task force should think of it this way: When does a change in methodology or delivery go beyond "just good teaching"? If a teacher does things a little differently for Carlos than she does for most students, is she doing what we would hope any good teacher would do? Or has it reached the point where it amounts to a change in methodology or delivery?

Have the task force divide all cited educational services as follows:

Just Good Teaching	*SDI due to Methodology or Delivery*

These lists may look different from one district to another. Also, consider that some services may be "just good teaching" if they are needed only occasionally, but may qualify as SDI if required regularly.

2

STEP TWO

STRUCTURE DECISION MAKING FROM THE BOTTOM UP.

Public education is very much a top-down system. The state legislatures create the legal framework, the school boards set the policies, the superintendents run the districts, and the principals are in charge of the campuses. Examples of the top-down nature of public education abound. Assistant principals often bear the brunt of it, enforcing rules that were not of their making. Teachers certainly understand that they are low on the totem pole, subject to the decisions of the people who occupy the multiple layers above them.

However, special ed is upside down. Decisions in special education must be based on the student's individual needs, as they are documented in the school's evaluation data. The most valuable evaluation data comes from those who have classroom experience with the student — the teachers. Therefore, the most legally defensible decisions are those that are strongly supported by the service providers. Educational leaders are wise to take this into account.

There are numerous examples to illustrate this point, but I think the best arise from two decisions from the 5th Circuit going back to the early days of special education litigation. *Crawford v. Pittman*, 708 F.2d 1028 (5th Cir. 1983) is a case in which the unique needs of a student with a disability trumped the clearly established top-down rule that limited students to 180 days of instruction. The parents of the student in this case sought an extension of services into the summer months. They claimed that with a three-month break in services, their child would lose whatever benefit he had gained from his education. So, they asked the school district to provide what we now call "extended school year" (ESY) services. The district balked, citing the state law that applied to all students that set the school year at 180 days. There is nothing more "top down" than a state law, and this one certainly seemed defensible because it did not discriminate against students with disabilities — they got 180 days of instruction just like everyone else.

But the court ruled in favor of the student. The unique, disability-based needs of this student trumped the state legislature. The court put it this way:

> *The issue is whether employees of a state that receives federal funds under [the predecessor to IDEA] may refuse, in formulating individual education programs (IEPs) for children within their school system, to consider the possible necessity for programs extending beyond 180 days per year. Reversing the district court, we hold that such a policy violates the Act's mandate that an*

individual educational program be designed to meet the personal needs of each handicapped child. The Act requires the state to treat each child as an individual, a human whose unique qualities and needs can be evaluated and served only by a plan designed with wisdom, care and educational expertise. Its grand design does not tolerate policies that impose a rigid pattern on the education of children. Each IEP must be prepared on the basis of an individual evaluation of a particular boy or girl. The child and his or her parents and guardians can exact no more. The state must provide no less.

The second case is *Alamo Heights ISD v. State Board of Education*, 790 F.2d 1153 (5th Cir. 1986). This was another ESY case, and the 5th Circuit affirmed its earlier ruling, thus requiring Alamo Heights ISD to serve the student in the summer months. But this case presented another top-down rule that the parents challenged: district boundaries. The case involved a student who required an after-school caretaker. According to the court, the only person the parents could find to provide care lived one mile beyond district boundaries. The parents' request for transportation services beyond district boundaries "was refused by school officials, without consultation with Steven's ARD Committee [the Texas version of an IEP team] or with his teacher."

Well, you can imagine how that happened. The transportation director and/or the principal most likely made the call. The decision, on the face of it, appears logical. It was not discriminatory; the district transported no one beyond district boundaries. Furthermore, the district probably had concerns about setting precedent: "If we grant this request, how many more will we receive?" So, the request was denied as a matter of top-down decision making.

However, the 5th Circuit said this was wrong, stating:

This analysis suggests that the "transportation" required as a "related service" under the Act is not arbitrarily limited by the geographic boundaries of the school district so long as it is required for the special circumstances of the handicapped child and is reasonable when all of the facts are considered.

Notice that what is normally a perfectly legitimate top-down rule is described by the court as an arbitrary limitation when it comes to a particular special education student. Again, decision making in special education must come from the bottom up. It should come from the IEP team and should reflect the team's careful consideration of the evaluation data. IEP team meetings should follow the IEP Team Decision-Making Pyramid:

As the Egyptians built the pyramids, so the IEP team should make decisions — from the bottom up. It is a good analogy, but one that should not be taken too literally. IEPs are supposed to last for one year, whereas the pyramids have been around for

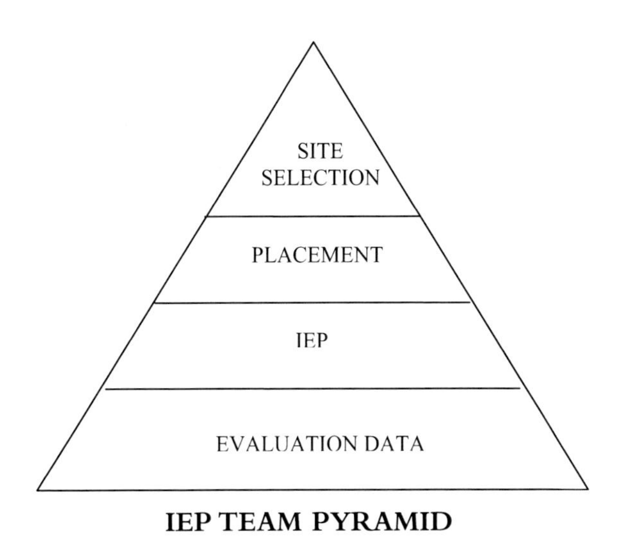

IEP TEAM PYRAMID

centuries. Moreover, you should be able to conduct your IEP team meeting in less time than it took to build the pyramids — and there should be no slave labor involved. But as far as working from the bottom up, it continues to be a good analogy.

3

STEP THREE

PROVIDE SDI TO GENERAL EDUCATION STUDENTS.

Special education never was intended to be for every student who has learning problems. As we have seen already, special education falls under SDI, but not all SDI qualifies as special education. Special education is SDI provided for a particular purpose: to "address the unique needs of the child that result from the disability." If you think about it, there are many students in your school who need SDI — changes in content, methodology or delivery of service — for a reason other than a disability. Thus, SDI can be provided to general education students.

Recent legislation makes it very clear that Congress believes that special education services can be strengthened by providing better services to those kids who need SDI for some other reason. I call them Quadrant III kids, based on this Four Quadrant Analysis:

	NO DISABILITY	HAS A DISABILITY
DOES NOT NEED SDI	I GENERAL ED	II 504
NEEDS SDI	III LEP SLOW LEARNERS WBFWR	IV SPECIAL EDUCATION IDEA ELIGIBLE

This analysis features the two criteria necessary for a student to be identified as eligible under IDEA: The student must 1) have a disability and 2) need SDI. If either of those factors are not present, the student is not eligible. These students occupy Quadrant IV in our Analysis.

Quadrant I includes those students who do not have a disability and do not need SDI. Very likely, your school's valedictorian is a Quadrant I student, as are most of the students in the top of your graduating class. But there are also many weaker students in Quadrant I. They may need extra help from time to time. They may fail a course or two.

They likely have strengths and weaknesses and will do well in some courses and not so well in others. But they can learn the general curriculum as set out by your state, and they do not need, on an ongoing basis, any changes in method or delivery of service. Thus, they belong in Quadrant I.

Quadrant II is for students eligible for some sort of services or accommodations under Section 504. Many educators believe that the difference between Section 504 and IDEA-eligible students is the severity of the disability. However, there is no support for that concept in the law. Both groups of students have serious disabilities, not minor problems. For special education (IDEA) purposes, we say that the disability must be such that it results in a need for SDI. Under Section 504, the language is different, but the result is much the same. To be eligible for services or accommodations under Section 504, the student's disability must *substantially impair* the student in a *major life activity*. Thus, the difference between these two laws is not a matter of severity; it has to do with what the student needs. If the student needs SDI due to his disability, he is IDEA eligible and we put him in Quadrant IV of our analysis. If the student's disability substantially impairs her in a major life activity but does not result in the need for SDI, then the student is 504 eligible — Quadrant II.

Quadrant III represents the students who are the focus of the No Child Left Behind Act and much of the reauthorization of IDEA. These are students who struggle in school and need some significant changes in content, methodology or delivery of instruction (read: SDI) — but not due to a disability.

The groups most likely found in Quadrant III would include LEP students (Limited English Proficient) and slow learners. A student who is learning English is going to need significant assistance to succeed in school in this country, but the student does not have a disability. Slow learners are those whose cognitive ability is well below average but not to the point of an intellectual disability. These kids are likely to need significant assistance in school, particularly as standards continue to ratchet up. But being below average is not a disability.

Perhaps the largest group in Quadrant III, however, are those we classify as WBFWR — Way Behind For Whatever Reason. There are many students whose difficulty in school can be attributed to non-disability factors, such as poverty, parental abuse or neglect or just general family dysfunction.

It is quite clear that Congress believes there are too many students in special education and that many of them are there for the wrong reasons. In IDEA 2004, Congress expressed a desire for stronger services to the kids in Quadrant III. They put it this way:

> Almost 30 years of research and experience has demonstrated that the education of children with disabilities can be made more effective by — providing incentives for whole-school approaches, scientifically based early-reading programs, positive behavioral interventions and supports, and early intervening services to reduce the need to label children as disabled in order to address the learning and behavioral needs of such children. 20 U.S.C. 1400(c)(5)(F)

Notice what they are saying: Give these kids the services they need, but do it outside of special education. In other words, give them SDI, but don't make them "special ed" to do so.

Why do we have too many kids in special ed? In no particular order, I would suggest the following factors:

1. Parent request/pressure
2. Accountability anxiety
3. We don't know where else to put them.
4. It's the only place where special help is available.
5. We fail to rule out other factors.

A number of steps can be taken to address this concern, and one of them is surely to provide the same services to general education students that you now provide to special education students. There is nothing in the law to prohibit this. In fact, IDEA 2004 encourages it. But there are two important limitations on that statement.

**For accountability purposes, the student must be tested on grade level, unless the student is in Quadrant IV.*

***As a general rule, federal funding under IDEA can only be spent on students in Quadrant IV.*

But these are the only limitations imposed by the law. As far as the services provided to students on a day-to-day basis, whatever you are doing for students in special education can be done for general education students. What you are doing in Quadrant IV can be done in Quadrant III.

How would this make your special education program more effective? It would focus it on the students who should be there. It relieves the strain of serving every struggling student. It reduces the tension between general ed and special ed staff. It might even quell the "border war" that goes on in many districts between Quadrant III and Quadrant IV. We see it all the time: General ed staff pushes Quadrant III kids over the border into IV, while diagnosticians, school psychologists and other special ed types fiercely resist. If everyone recognized responsibility for kids who are having a hard time in school, it might solve a lot of problems.

4

STEP FOUR

CREATE A STRONG EARLY INTERVENTION TEAM ON EVERY CAMPUS.

Once educators truly come to believe that SDI can be provided to general education students, they will need to put a structure in place to make sure that this happens. That structure is your campus-based early intervention team.

This group used to be called the "pre-referral team" and still may be called that on some campuses. While the law does not dictate a name for this group, I prefer "early intervention." The term "pre-referral" makes it sound like this is simply a necessary speed bump on the way to a special education referral. The "pre-referral" team would meet, check off all the necessary boxes and initiate the referral for special education testing.

Zip zap — now on to Quadrant IV!

That is not how it is supposed to work. The early intervention team should be a group that is knowledgeable of the Four Quadrant Analysis. They should be familiar with all of the special services — all of the SDI services — that are available on campus. They should meet on a regular basis to consider those students who are having difficulty in Quadrant I. The early intervention team is responsible for coming up with educational plans for these students.

The customary process for pre-referral teams has been to assess a student one time only, with no intention to monitor the student's progress. This makes sense if the only function of the pre-referral process is to lay the groundwork for a special education referral. But with changes in the law over the past few years, it has become clear that the early intervention team should not only develop an individualized plan for a student, but then also monitor the success of that plan. The team also should do this for all students who are going to stay outside of Quadrant IV.

These changes in the law have happened at the national level. The national changes are embodied in IDEA 2004 and its emphasis on early intervention, school-wide strategies and positive behavior programs, all of which are designed to improve student performance for the kids in Quadrant III. NCLB reinforces this by requiring the disaggregation of data in the testing program. This puts the focus on the success of groups of students who are disproportionately in Quadrant III (LEP, low income).

The point, once again, is that SDI is not limited to special education students. For those students who are not in special education, the early intervention team could serve as well as an IEP team does in creating plans, monitoring their effectiveness and making changes as situations dictate.

5

STEP FIVE

USE GOALS AND MEASURING STICKS PEOPLE CAN UNDERSTAND.

If you decided to lose 15 pounds over the next six months, how would you know if you were successful? If you decided to put aside $100 per month in savings, how would you know if you were successful?

When we consider these common examples of goal setting, we see that measuring success can be very simple. If my plan is to lose a certain amount of weight over a certain period of time, all I need is a scale and a calendar. At the end of six months, I step on the scale and — *Voila*! I have either met the goal or not. The same is true with our money-saving goal. All I need is a bank account and a calendar.

The goals in a student's IEP should be just as clear and just as easily measured. The law calls for an IEP to include 1) where academically the student is now; 2) where academically the student will be in one year; and 3) how we will know if we have reached the desired outcome. The terminology used in the law is:

WHERE NOW: present levels of academic achievement and functional performance

WHERE IN ONE YEAR: measurable annual goals, including academic and functional goals

HOW TO KNOW: a description of how the child's progress toward meeting the annual goals will be measured.
20 U.S.C. 1414(d)(1)(A)(i)(I-III)

My personal observation is that the lower the student is functioning, the more measurable the goals are and the simpler the measuring stick is. I once saw an IEP goal that called for the student to "toss a beanbag into a hula hoop from a distance of 10 feet on seven out of 10 trials." Give me the student, a beanbag, a hula hoop and a tape measure, and I will tell you if the goal has been achieved. The measuring stick is simple. The goal is measurable. A goal is measurable if an outside person, knowing nothing about the school or the student, can look at your data and tell you whether or not the goal has been achieved.

Parents are clamoring for clear-cut, easily measured goals. Passing the grade-level, statewide accountability test is a simple and objectively measurable goal. Making a specific amount of progress as measured by an instrument, such as Brigance screens, is measurable. "Making measurable progress in reading and language arts" is not clear, not objective and not measurable.

The law does not expect every child to achieve every goal every year. But it does expect every goal to be written in such a way that it is clear whether or not the student has met the goal.

6

STEP SIX

ASSEMBLE A STRONG TEAM OF EXPERTS.

My first experience with "experts" was with Catholic priests. I grew up in a big city neighborhood where almost everyone was Catholic. We had a huge parish with about eight or 10 priests. Confessions were heard every Saturday, and we children quickly learned that there were some priests we would rather go to, and some we would not. I usually sought out Father Stevens. No matter what sins I committed or how many times I committed them, Father Stevens seemed unperturbed, unruffled. He was neither disappointed in me, nor was he harsh. I liked him. He became "my priest."

I now choose a wide variety of experts: doctors, dentists, accountants, car mechanics, computer geeks. I find that I am always looking for the same qualities. I want someone who is competent, of course, but many other qualities are important as well. They must communicate well, and in a nontechnical way. They must care about my long-term best interests. They must advise me of the pros and cons, but then let me make the decisions. I want to feel that they are "on my side." But they must tell me hard facts when I need to hear them; I don't want them to sugarcoat things or lie to me.

The school should be looking for the same things as it creates a stable of experts to assist with the special education program. Experts of all kinds are needed. This includes experts on instructional strategies, behavior programs, autism, medical problems, reading — the list goes on and on. As pointed out earlier, evaluation data is crucial. It is the rudder that steers the ship. Decision making should be based on evaluation data. While much of that evaluation data comes from the classroom teacher, there is a crucial role to be played by the expert who is not regularly employed by the school but is brought in as a consultant.

One of the first autism cases I dealt with happened in a very small school district. Crystal (not her real name) presented a host of problems, and frankly, the district had no experience or expertise in working with students like her. I was brought in to defend the district in a due process hearing. I made one very good decision at the beginning of the case. I advised the district to hire an expert on autism to evaluate our program and advise us. I told the district, right from the start, that we were going to base our case on this expert. If she told us we were doing things wrong, we would change. If that meant we had to settle the case, we would settle the case. If she thought our program was good, she would become our key witness.

After evaluating the school's program, the expert concluded that the district was doing some things well, but she did make suggestions to change certain things. We followed her advice. She testified in support of the district. The hearing officer ruled for the district. I am convinced that would not have happened had we not brought in an expert who was not regularly employed by the district.

Choosing the experts who will evaluate the student is crucial. There is much room for subjectivity and professional judgment when it comes to special education. Eligibility criteria alone present a good example. The definition of "seriously emotionally disturbed" (SED), for example, leaves considerable room for reputable experts to reach different conclusions from the same data. The definition of SED requires the student to demonstrate certain characteristics "over a long period of time and to a marked degree" but neither "long" nor "marked" are further quantified or defined. Moreover, the characteristics include such nebulous terms as:

"an inability to build or maintain satisfactory interpersonal relationships with peers and teachers"

"inappropriate types of behavior or feelings under normal circumstances"

Then, there is my favorite:

"a general pervasive mood of unhappiness or depression"

Looking at the same data and the same student, one psychologist might find an emotional disturbance while another finds a typical adolescent. One may conclude that the student is taking drugs because she is depressed and, therefore, SED; while another may believe she is depressed because she is taking drugs and, therefore, is not SED. Both experts are honest, reputable and relying on valid data. The problem is that there are many judgment calls to be made. Special education is not a precise science.

Therefore, choosing experts who are compatible with and supportive of the school district's philosophy is very important. They will be creating and interpreting much of the evaluation data, which is, as you will recall, the basis for decision making, the foundation of the pyramid and the rudder that steers the ship.

Moreover, this is one area in which the law is, as the lawyers like to say, "well settled." The school district has the discretion to choose which experts it will rely upon. It has the authority to decide which experts will conduct evaluations of students. This first came up in *Andress v. Cleveland ISD*, 64 F.3d 176 (5th Cir. 1995). In that case, the parents of a student objected to the school's plan to conduct an evaluation using school personnel. The parents had had the child evaluated independently, by someone they chose, and they demanded that the school rely on that evaluation rather than conducting its own. The court's ruling in favor of the school was unmistakably clear:

If a student's parents want him to receive special education under IDEA, they must allow the school itself to reevaluate the student and they cannot force the school to rely solely on an independent evaluation.

Therefore, we hold that there is no exception to the rule that a school district has a right to test a student itself in order to evaluate or reevaluate the student's eligibility under IDEA.

Thus, this is an area where the law is not at all murky. Schools can choose their experts and can rely on those experts in making educational decisions. So, research a complete array of experts and choose them wisely.

7

STEP SEVEN

USE BIPs TO SUPPLEMENT — NOT SUPPLANT —YOUR STUDENT CODE OF CONDUCT.

More parents go to due process hearings over discipline issues than anything else. There is no area of special education law more complicated, or more controversial, than discipline. To operate an effective program, school administrators must have a clear understanding of what the law allows and what the law prohibits.

All too often, however, school administrators and teachers are confused about the law. One of the primary manifestations of this is the commonly held belief that a student who has a behavior intervention plan (BIP) is no longer subject to the Student Code of Conduct. A BIP is not a substitute for the conduct code; it is an addition to it.

Some IEP forms contribute to the problem by asking this question:

> *Can the student follow the Code of Conduct?*
>
> If "yes," then the Student Code of Conduct applies. If "no," then the ARD Committee must write a BIP as a substitute for the Student Code of Conduct.

But this is fundamentally wrong. The question is irrelevant, impossible to answer and not supported in the law. The more appropriate question is the one the law tells us to ask:

> *Does the student have behaviors that impede learning of the student or others?*
>
> If "yes," then consider positive behavioral

interventions, supports and strategies—such as a BIP—to address those behaviors.

Both the Student Code of Conduct and the BIP are designed to promote appropriate student behavior, but they go about it in very different ways. There are five fundamental differences between a Student Code of Conduct and a BIP.

Student Code of Conduct	BIP
Negative	Positive
Reactive	Proactive
Applies to all	Applies to one student
Imposed by the school	Agreed to by the school and parent
What the school does TO the student	What the school does FOR the student

Negative vs. Positive

The Student Code of Conduct is full of negative consequences. The concept of due process of law requires that public schools give students notice of the types of behavior for which they might be punished and the types of punishments that are available. The Student Code of Conduct serves as the school's official written notice. The code informs students of what behaviors or actions might result in a three-day suspension, a trip to an alternative disciplinary program or an expulsion. It is a menu of negative consequences that are designed to promote positive student behavior. The theory is that the fear of negative consequences will motivate students to behave appropriately. With most kids, this works. So the Student Code of Conduct, similar to your state's penal code, is focused on negative consequences for negative behavior.

IDEA requires that a BIP be positive. IDEA does not dictate what a BIP is supposed to look like, how long it should be or how it is written. But it does require that the BIP include "positive behavioral interventions and supports." 20 U.S.C. 1414(d)(3)(B)(i).

Reactive vs. Proactive

No one bothers to study the Student Code of Conduct until a student misbehaves. When a student is sent to the assistant principal's office and a transgression is reported, the assistant principal should consult the Student Code of Conduct to determine the consequence that applies. The sequence of events is:

1. Student misbehaves.
2. Assistant principal consults Student Code of Conduct.

So the code is used in a *reactive* way, to *respond* to student misconduct.

A BIP, on the other hand, should describe the interventions and strategies the school will use on a regular basis to deter the student from engaging in certain behaviors. Let us take a more complete look at the language in the law.

> *The IEP team shall:*
>
> *(i) in the case of a child whose behavior impedes the child's learning or that of others, consider the use of positive behavioral interventions and supports, and other strategies, to address that behavior.*
>
> 20 U.S.C. 1414(d)(3)(B)(i)

Thus the sequence of events is:

1. IEP team identifies behaviors that impede learning.
2. IEP team develops a BIP to address the targeted behaviors.

3. School staff members use the "intervention and supports" to reduce or eliminate the targeted behaviors.

Applies to All vs. Applies to One

The Student Code of Conduct applies to all students without exception, whereas a BIP is crafted for one student only. A code is a blunt instrument that calls for certain consequences for misconduct without taking into account the individual circumstances of the student. To sharpen that blunt instrument just a bit, most schools have adopted policies that give school administrators and teachers some degree of discretion in applying the code. Thus, applying the code is not simply a mechanical process. Nevertheless, it applies to all students, just as residency and vaccination requirements apply to all students. There is nothing in IDEA or state law that exempts students with disabilities from the application of the Student Code of Conduct.

A BIP, on the other hand, is individually crafted by the student's IEP team. The plan targets the student's problematic behaviors and outlines strategies and interventions designed specifically for that student. It is a sharp instrument.

Imposed by the School vs. Agreed to by the School and the Parents

Parents and students are not asked to agree to the Student Code of Conduct. They are asked to sign a statement to indicate that they have read it. The code is usually developed by educators and approved by a school board. Of course parents who wish to be involved in that process can do so, but the fact of the matter is that the Code is developed by the people who run the school and then imposed on students and parents. Parents have a fundamental constitutional right to direct the upbringing of their children, but that right does not extend so far as to allow them to dictate the details of school disciplinary policies.

A BIP, on the other hand, is a key component of a student's IEP. A BIP must be developed by the student's IEP team, which includes the parent(s). Thus, the school cannot dictate the terms of a BIP; it must seek consensus with the parent.

This fundamental distinction between codes of conduct and BIPs leads to two specific suggestions:

1. Don't propose "interventions and strategies" in a BIP that already are contained in the Student Code of Conduct and, thus, do not require parental agreement. "Calling the police" in the event a student commits a crime is the best example of this. Your Student Code of Conduct already says that you will do this. You do not need parental agreement to do this, so why ask for parental agreement when you do not need it? How will you

respond if you propose this in a BIP and the parent does not agree?

2. Don't enumerate in a BIP all of the short-term disciplinary consequences already listed in the Student Code of Conduct. Federal law requires IEP Team action prior to any *long-term* disciplinary action that amounts to a *change of placement*. Short-term consequences — such as a few days of suspension or in-school suspension or the withdrawal of privileges — can be imposed without IEP Team action. If your proposed BIP includes such "interventions and strategies" as "ISS for three days," you effectively are asking the parents to approve something the school already has the authority to use. You are limiting the use of the code with the student.

To the Student vs. For the Student

Perhaps this is what best sums up the point I am trying to make. Codes of conduct and BIPs should work together, sort of like a "good cop/bad cop" scenario. A BIP describes what the school will do *for* the student in an effort to reduce, eliminate or replace inappropriate behaviors. Like any other educational service, a BIP is designed to teach, motivate, encourage and reinforce positive behaviors.

The Student Code of Conduct is the "bad cop," waiting in the wings if the BIP does not produce the desired results. Suppose, for example, that the BIP addresses the student's problem with anger management. The BIP includes positive interventions and supports designed to teach the student how to control his behavior when provoked. But three weeks after the BIP is introduced, the student flies into a rage, curses at the teacher and throws a book against the wall.

The student has violated the Student Code of Conduct and is subject to possible disciplinary action. Of course, if this happens repeatedly (the law has a 10-day standard), the IEP team should get together to consider revisions to the BIP. To carry our analogy just a step farther, if we have to rely on the "bad cop" too often, we need to get a better "good cop."

Special education directors are very familiar with the phrase "supplement, not supplant," which is commonly used regarding federally funded programs. Federal funds must be used to supplement — not supplant — other funding. Consider adopting the same mindset with regard to codes of conduct and BIPs. The BIP does not substitute for the code; it supplements it.

8

STEP EIGHT

HAVE STRONG LEADERSHIP AT YOUR IEP TEAM MEETINGS.

The IEP team meeting is the critical vehicle for school/parent communication. How the meeting is conducted speaks volumes about the professionalism and caring of the school district. It is essential that the meeting have strong leadership.

Federal law requires that school districts initiate and conduct IEP meetings. Parents have the opportunity to participate as equal partners in the process, but it is not the parents' meeting. The meeting is about a particular student, but it is not the student's meeting. It is the school's meeting, which means that the school bears primary responsibility for the quality of the meeting.

IEP team meetings are unique to special education, but in many respects, they are like any other meeting. Any meeting that lacks focus is likely to be unproductive. Any meeting without a clearly defined objective is likely to go nowhere. Any meeting participant who does not understand what is going on is likely to leave the meeting feeling frustrated.

All of this means that the IEP team needs a strong leader. A strong leader sets the tone for the meeting, establishes and enforces "ground rules" for productive discussion, and makes sure that all voices are heard, all issues are addressed and decisions are made in an orderly fashion.

The IEP team leader must have good people skills and good communications skills, but he or she does not have to be the leading expert on special education law in your district. The IEP team leader should have a solid understanding of what IEP team meetings are about, but knowing the specific details of federal or state regulations is not a requirement.

The most logical person to serve as the IEP team leader is a "representative of the local educational agency." Federal law dictates who is to serve on the team. Among the required members is:

> *(iii) a representative of the local educational agency who —*
>
> > *(I) is qualified to provide, or supervise the provision of, specially designed instruction to meet the unique needs of children with disabilities;*
> >
> > *(II) is knowledgeable about the general curriculum; and*
> >
> > *(III) is knowledgeable about the availability of resources of the local educational agency.*
> >
> > 20 U.S.C. 1414(d)(1)(B)(iv)

Historically, this person has been the one who has had the authority to commit agency resources and ensure that the services set out in the IEP are actually provided. In the 1999 version of the regulations, Appendix A made this explicit:

> *Each public agency may determine which specific staff member will serve as the agency representative in a particular IEP meeting, so long as the individual meets these requirements. It is important, however, that the agency representative have the authority to commit agency resources and be able to ensure that whatever services are set out in the IEP will actually be provided.* 34 C.F.R. 300, Appendix A, Question 22

Thus, the person we customarily would call the "administrative representative" could be filled by a local educational agency representative who has the authority to commit the school to the plan. With that authority should come the responsibility to serve as the IEP team leader.

In too many school districts, the educational diagnostician or school psychologist is called on to play too many roles at the meeting. This individual is frequently required to fill out all the paperwork, lead the discussion, establish rapport with the parents, etc. A more well-run IEP team meeting calls on each person to take on a role that best suits their expertise and abilities. This would free up the diagnostician or similar "special ed type" to address all the paperwork and compliance issues, while the administrative representative focuses on leading the team meetings.

While there are many people around the table at an IEP team meeting, there are really only two parties: the parent (or adult student) and the school. The administrative representative is the highest ranking school official at the meeting, and is empowered with the authority to commit the resources of the district. As such, he or she is the logical leader for the school and for the meeting as a whole.

9

STEP NINE

WORK EFFECTIVELY WITH YOUR LAWYER.

You may consider the lawyers you work with a necessary evil. I hope not. I hope you consider your lawyer a part of the team. At the Walsh Anderson Law Firm, we strive to live by our motto: HELPING THE PEOPLE WHO HELP THE KIDS.

Are lawyers a "necessary evil"? Let's examine that one word at a time. Are they necessary? Yes. Educational policy with regard to students with disabilities became a matter of federal law more than 30 years ago. The sheer volume of laws, regulations and important cases has only mushroomed since then. Routinely, I have suggested that school districts should never allow an IEP team meeting to conclude without a consensus unless the school district can answer "yes" to these three questions:

1. Is this something worth fighting over?
2. Is the school staff united?
3. *Are we legally defensible?*

If you are going to have a disagreement with a parent, it is likely to play out in the legal arena, so Question 3 becomes quite important. And Question 3 should be answered by your lawyer. So, yes, lawyers are "necessary."

Lawyers are not "evil." A school district's attorney has a tremendous opportunity to serve the greater good. By providing sound legal advice that is focused on the long-term interests of the client, the school attorney also serves the interests of parents and students. Any advice aimed at the school's long-term interest is advice designed to avoid problems. Yet, the aim is higher than that. Schools avoid problems by complying with the law, communicating effectively with parents and serving students as well as possible.

School lawyers should not dictate educational policy. The role of the lawyer is to advise about pros and cons, risks and rewards. But in doing so, the lawyer, if used effectively, can help the district ensure compliance, avoid legal disputes when possible and prevail in those that cannot be avoided.

So, here are the basic rules for using your lawyer effectively:

1. Get a good one. Special education law is complex. Establish a relationship with a lawyer who devotes a goodly amount of his or her practice to special education. As the client, you should interview your lawyer to ascertain that he or she has the level of experience and knowledge that you deserve.

There are many very fine lawyers out there who would not know an IEP from a PIE. Stay away from them.

2. Establish an ongoing relationship. Many law firms now offer low-cost "retainer programs," designed to encourage districts to get preventive advice over the telephone before trouble gets out of hand. Take advantage of one of these. An ongoing relationship with your lawyer is helpful because the lawyer gets to know the people, the programs and the problems of the district, all of which enables the lawyer to give better advice.
3. Choose one lawyer or firm. Fortunately, there are many good lawyers and firms that focus on this area of the law. But it is counterproductive for a district to seek advice from more than one source. Some districts have retainer agreements with multiple law firms, and this can lead to a

dysfunctional situation. Competent lawyers can hear the same question and answer it quite differently. It is not helpful if Firm A says one thing and Firm B says something else. Choose one.

4. Choose your lawyer as you choose any other expert. See the discussion above about the choice of educational experts. Because of the confidentiality and sensitivity of many legal matters, it is even more important that your lawyer be a person who is philosophically compatible with your district and personally comfortable with key staff in your district.
5. Do not shop for advice. A good lawyer does not always tell you what you want to hear.
6. Disclose all relevant facts. A lawyer's advice is always dependent on the facts. You have to supply the facts. If you give the lawyer erroneous facts or leave out important facts, the advice you receive will not be sound.

Of course, this is a two-way responsibility. A good lawyer probes and asks relevant questions so that he or she gets a good understanding of the facts. But as the client, you must do your part as well.

7. Identify the people in the district who are authorized to get legal advice for the district. This is a suggestion designed to keep your legal bills under control. It also will help you avoid the dysfunctional situation in which two or more people independently ask for advice about the same situation. It is highly unlikely that the special education director and the personnel director will ask exactly the same question or provide exactly the same background information. Consequently, they may not get the same answer. Problems ensue. Streamline and control the process.
8. Do let the lawyer know what you would like to do. A lawyer should never give into

the temptation to simply tell the client what the client wants to hear for the sake of expedience. But it is a lawyer's job to help the client accomplish his or her goals without undue legal risk. So spell it out. Tell the lawyer your destination, and let the lawyer help you get there.

9. Do not get off the phone until you understand. There are many subtle distinctions in the law, and legal advice is often misconstrued or misunderstood. Lawyers should do their part to make the advice as clear-cut as possible, but clients have a responsibility as well. If you do not understand, say so. If you want it in writing, authorize it. If you think you understand and then realize 15 minutes later that you do not, call back.

10. Call early. When you see storm clouds headed your way, call your lawyer. Do not wait until the thunder rumbles, the

lightning flashes, and the hail dents your car.

11. Use lawyers for staff development. It is helpful for all school staff to have a basic understanding of what the law requires. Certainly the special education staff and administrators need to know about the law. Consider bringing in your school attorney or special education attorney to do some in-service work.
12. Remember who the lawyer represents. The school district's lawyer does not represent you. The school district's lawyer represents the school district — a faceless, governmental entity. The school district's lawyer is supposed to look out for the best interests of the school district — not any of the individuals who work for the school district. Moreover, the special education lawyer does not represent the special ed department — the lawyer represents the school district as a whole.

10

STEP TEN

KEEP A LONG-TERM PERSPECTIVE.

It is easy to get frustrated with the plethora of legal requirements in special education, not to mention the conflicts and stress that accompany them. It is important, and encouraging, to step back from time to time and reflect on just how far we've come. Here is a brief synopsis of some key moments in the history of American public education.

1777 Thomas Jefferson proposes a plan for public education in Virginia that would include a scholarship for 20 male students in Virginia. The boy selected would be "of the best and most promising genius and disposition." Jefferson defended his plan by noting:

"By this means 20 of the best geniuses will be

raked from the rubbish annually and instructed at public expense."

1840 Horace Mann advocates virtue. In his annual report to the Massachusetts Legislature in 1840, Mann had this to say about the responsibility of the "school committee," which, in today's parlance, would be the school board.

"In the contemplation of the law, the school committee are sentinels stationed at the door of every schoolhouse in the state to see that no teacher ever crosses its threshold who is not clothed from the crown of his head to the sole of his feet in garments of virtue."

1954 The Supreme Court reminds us of the importance of education.

"Today, education is perhaps the most important function of state and local

governments. Compulsory school attendance laws and the great expenditures for education both demonstrate our recognition of the importance of education to our democratic society. It is required in the performance of our most basic public responsibilities, even service in the armed forces. It is the very foundation of good citizenship. Today it is a principal instrument in awakening the child to cultural values, in preparing him for later professional training and in helping him to adjust normally to his environment. In these days, it is doubtful that any child may reasonably be expected to succeed in life if he is denied the opportunity of an education. Such an opportunity, where the state has undertaken to provide it, is a right which must be made available to all on equal terms." Brown v. Board of Education of Topeka, 74 S. Ct. 686 (1954).

1955 Rosa Parks takes her seat on the bus.

1957? Mrs. Gump tries to get Forrest enrolled in school.

1975 President Gerald Ford signs the first federal special education law and makes a prediction:

Unfortunately, this bill promises more than the Federal Government can deliver, and the many unwise provisions it contains could thwart its good intentions. Everyone can agree with the objective stated in the title of this bill, "educating all handicapped children in our Nation." The key question is whether the bill will really accomplish that objective.

Even the strongest supporters of this measure know as well as I that they are falsely raising the expectations of the groups affected by claiming authorization levels that are excessive and unrealistic.

Despite my strong support for full educational opportunities for our handicapped children, the funding levels proposed in this bill will simply not be possible if federal expenditures are to be brought under control and a balanced budget achieved over the next few years.

There are other features in the bill which I believe to be objectionable and which should be changed. It contains a vast array of detailed, complex and costly administrative requirements, which would unnecessarily assert federal control over traditional state and local government functions. It establishes complex requirements under which tax dollars would be used to support administrative paperwork and not educational programs. Unfortunately, these requirements will remain in effect even though the Congress appropriates far less than the amounts contemplated in [the law]. Public Papers of the Presidents; 1975, Book II, pages 1935-1936.

From the perspective of 2012, we can see that much of what President Ford predicted has come to pass. Special education programs are still over-regulated, complex, paperwork-intensive and drastically under-funded. But millions of kids are receiving services that would not have been provided in the past. Schools are serving students with more severe disabilities in more mainstream settings.

The law has evolved. Laws always answer questions, but when you study the evolution of our special education laws, you can see that the questions have changed as the services to students have improved.

Let me illustrate. In 1975, the original version of what we now call IDEA answered two fundamental questions:

Question	*Answer*
WHO must be served?	ALL students, no matter how severe.
WHERE to serve them?	In the LRE as much as possible.

By 1997, when the law was reauthorized, there was a new question to be answered:

Question	*Answer*
WHAT to teach them?	The GENERAL CURRICULUM (in other words, the same as we teach other students)

With the 2004 version of the law, along with NCLB, we have a question that challenges our expectations for these students:

Question	*Answer*
What should we EXPECT from them?	THE SAME as we expect from other students.

LET'S SUMMARIZE

I encourage you to take these 10 key steps, which I believe will improve your program and services.

1. Get your staff to define what is and is not "special education" in your district.
2. Structure decision making from the bottom up.
3. Provide specially designed instruction (SDI) to the general education students who need it.
4. Create and support a strong early intervention team on every campus.

5. Use goals and measuring sticks people can understand.
6. Assemble a valuable team of experts.
7. Use BIPs to supplement your Student Code of Conduct, not to supplant it.
8. Have strong leadership at your IEP team meetings.
9. Work effectively with your lawyer.
10. Keep your perspective!

Jim Walsh, publisher and managing editor of *Texas School Administrators' Legal Digest*, is one of the founding members of Walsh, Anderson, Gallegos, Green & Treviño, which represents many school districts and other educational entities in Texas and New Mexico. A 1975 graduate of the University of Texas School of Law, Walsh is the co-author of *The Educator's Guide to Texas School Law* and the author of *This Just In...*, a monthly newsletter on special education. He has taught school law at Baylor University and Texas State University and has conducted in-service training sessions at every Education Service Center in the state and for hundreds of school districts.